TABLE OF CONTENTS

CHAPTER 1

ROCKY WONDERS

Welcome to Türkiye! Would you like to explore an **ancient** city? Part of Cappadocia was carved from rock. People have lived in this area for more than 2,500 years!

Cappadocia

ALL AROUND THE WORLD
TÜRKIYE

by Kristine Spanier, MLIS

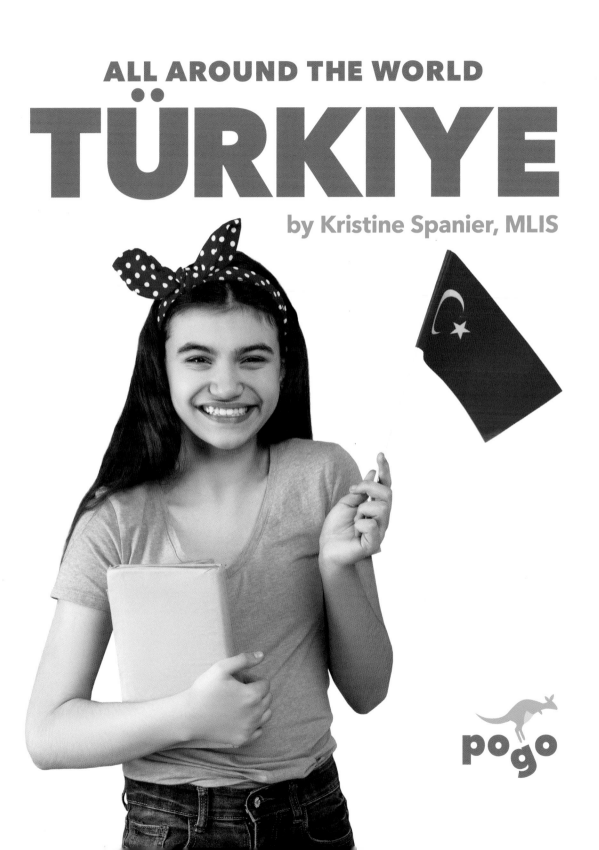

pogo

Ideas for Parents and Teachers

Pogo Books let children practice reading informational text while introducing them to nonfiction features such as headings, labels, sidebars, maps, and diagrams, as well as a table of contents, glossary, and index.

Carefully leveled text with a strong photo match offers early fluent readers the support they need to succeed.

Before Reading

- "Walk" through the book and point out the various nonfiction features. Ask the student what purpose each feature serves.
- Look at the glossary together. Read and discuss the words.

Read the Book

- Have the child read the book independently.
- Invite him or her to list questions that arise from reading.

After Reading

- Discuss the child's questions. Talk about how he or she might find answers to those questions.
- Prompt the child to think more. Ask: Türkiye's government honors children every year. Is there a holiday for children where you live? Do you think there should be? Why or why not?

Pogo Books are published by Jump!
5357 Penn Avenue South
Minneapolis, MN 55419
www.jumplibrary.com

Library of Congress Cataloging-in-Publication Data

Names: Spanier, Kristine, author.
Title: Türkiye / by Kristine Spanier, MLIS.
Description: Minneapolis, MN: Jump!, [2023]
Series: All around the world | Includes index.
Audience: Ages 7–10
Identifiers: LCCN 2022028373 (print)
LCCN 2022028374 (ebook)
ISBN 9798885242127 (hardcover)
ISBN 9798885242134 (paperback)
ISBN 9798885242141 (ebook)
Subjects: LCSH: Turkey–Juvenile literature.
Classification: LCC DR417.4 .S63 2023 (print)
LCC DR417.4 (ebook)
DDC 956.1–dc23/eng/20220622
LC record available at https://lccn.loc.gov/2022028373
LC ebook record available at https://lccn.loc.gov/2022028374

Editor: Jenna Gleisner
Designer: Molly Ballanger

Photo Credits: Nick N A/Shutterstock, cover; Prostock-studio/Shutterstock, 1; Pixfiction/Shutterstock, 3; Guitar photographer/Shutterstock, 4; prmustafa/iStock, 5; Hikrcn/Dreamstime, 6–7; Naeblys/Shutterstock, 8–9; Bilal Kocabas/Shutterstock, 10; railway fx/Shutterstock, 11 (flag); Pyty/Shutterstock, 11 (map); ADEM ALTAN/AFP/Getty, 12–13; Neliyana Kostadinova/Shutterstock, 14 (grape leaves); Picture Partners/Shutterstock, 14 (olives); Resul Muslu/Shutterstock, 14 (Turkish delight); erkan kurt/Dreamstime, 15; Cagkan Sayin/Shutterstock, 16–17; Artur Bogacki/Shutterstock, 18–19 (left); muratart/Shutterstock, 18–19 (right); Yasin AKGUL/AFP/Getty, 20–21; daphnusia images/Shutterstock, 23.

Printed in the United States of America at Corporate Graphics in North Mankato, Minnesota.

Natural **springs** and **minerals** create terraces in Pamukkale. "Pamukkale" is Turkish for "cotton castle." People have come to visit for more than 2,000 years. Some float in the waters.

terrace

Istanbul

Türkiye is a **land bridge**. It connects Europe and Asia. The city of Istanbul is in both!

The Aegean Sea is west. The Black Sea is north. The Mediterranean Sea is south. Türkiye has about 5,000 miles (8,000 kilometers) of coastline.

DID YOU KNOW?

Two major rivers flow through Türkiye. One is the Euphrates River. The other is the Tigris River. People travel on them. Farmers also use the water for **crops**.

Mount Ararat is in the east. This mountain has two peaks. Little Ararat is 12,782 feet (3,896 meters) high. Great Ararat is 16,945 feet (5,165 m) high. It is the tallest peak in Türkiye.

Great Ararat

Little Ararat

CHAPTER 2

TÜRKIYE'S LEADERS

In 2021, Türkiye's leaders changed the country's name. It used to be Turkey. The people of Türkiye vote for a president. This leader lives and works in Ankara. This is the **capital**.

Ankara

Türkiye joined the **North Atlantic Treaty Organization (NATO)** in 1952. NATO helps protect the freedom of the countries that are members.

NATO flag

■ = NATO countries

The Grand National Assembly makes laws. The group first met on April 23, 1920. That day, the president spoke about the children of Türkiye. Now, National **Sovereignty** and Children's Day is every April 23. Children gather in Ankara.

TAKE A LOOK!

The crescent moon and star on the Turkish flag are **symbols** of **Islam**. They have other meanings as well. What are they? Take a look!

■ = soldiers
☾ = religion
☆ = many **cultures**

CHAPTER 3

LIFE IN TÜRKIYE

Turkish foods are flavorful. Meze is a tray of appetizers. People share the food. Stuffed grape leaves and olives might be on it. Turkish delight is a chewy candy. It comes in many flavors.

olives

stuffed grape leaves

Turkish delight

Students learn other languages as early as first grade. Many choose English. They can also learn German, French, or Spanish.

Nearly half of the land here is used for farming. Cotton, fruits, and nuts are important crops. Farmers also grow barley, corn, and potatoes.

Many people make cloth, rugs, or clothes. Others build cars and electronics.

WHAT DO YOU THINK?

People visit Türkiye's beaches and cities. About half of the Turkish people work in **service jobs**. Many help those who visit. Do you think it would be fun working with visitors? Why or why not?

hazelnuts

dome

The Hagia Sophia was completed in 537. It is a **mosque** in Istanbul. The largest dome is 100 feet (30 m) across. It rises 180 feet (55 m).

WHAT DO YOU THINK?

The Hagia Sophia is one of Türkiye's most popular places for visitors. Some parts are closed during times of prayer. Do you think this is a good rule? Why or why not?

Have you ever seen whirling dervishes? These are Turkish dancers. They perform in a sema. This is a religious ceremony. The dancers wear long robes and tall hats. They whirl in circles to music.

There is a lot to see in Türkiye! Do you want to visit?

QUICK FACTS & TOOLS

AT A GLANCE

TÜRKIYE

Location: southeastern Europe and southwestern Asia

Size: 302,535 square miles (783,562 square kilometers)

Population: 83,047,706 (2022 estimate)

Capital: Ankara

Type of Government: presidential republic

Languages: Turkish (official), Kurdish

Exports: cars and vehicle parts, petroleum, jewelry, clothing

Currency: lira

GLOSSARY

ancient: Belonging to a period long ago.

capital: A city where government leaders meet.

crops: Plants grown for food.

cultures: The ideas, customs, traditions, and ways of life of groups of people.

Islam: The religion based on the teachings of Muhammad.

land bridge: A strip of land that connects two landmasses.

minerals: Naturally occurring substances in the ground.

mosque: A building in which Muslims worship.

North Atlantic Treaty Organization (NATO):
An organization of countries that have agreed to give each other military help. This group includes the United States, Canada, and some countries in Europe.

service jobs: Jobs and work that provide services for others, such as hotel, restaurant, and retail positions.

sovereignty: Supreme authority or the power to rule.

springs: Places where water rises to the surface from an underground source.

symbols: Objects or designs that stand for, suggest, or represent something else.

Türkiye's currency

INDEX

TO LEARN MORE

Finding more information is as easy as 1, 2, 3.

❶ Go to www.factsurfer.com

❷ Enter "Turkiye" into the search box.

❸ Choose your book to see a list of websites.

FACT SURFER